Make Your Own

Room Alarm

Julia Garstecki and
Stephanie Derkovitz

BLACK
RABBIT
BOOKS

Hi Jinx is published by Black Rabbit Books
P.O. Box 3263, Mankato, Minnesota, 56002.
www.blackrabbitbooks.com
Copyright © 2020 Black Rabbit Books

Marysa Storm, editor; Michael Sellner, designer;
Omay Ayres, photo researcher

Names: Garstecki, Julia, author. | Derkovitz,
Stephanie, author.
Title: Make your own room alarm / by Julia Garstecki
and Stephanie Derkovitz.
Description: Mankato, Minnesota : Hi Jinx/Black Rabbit
Books, [2020] | Series: Hi jinx. Make your own fun |
Includes bibliographical references and index. | Audience:
Ages 9-12. | Audience: Grades 4 to 6.
Identifiers: LCCN 2018033599 (print) | LCCN 2018037518
(ebook) | ISBN 9781680729429 (ebook) | ISBN
9781680729368 (library binding) |
ISBN 9781644660676 (paperback)
Subjects: LCSH: Electronic alarm systems–Design and
construction—Juvenile literature.
Classification: LCC TH9739 (ebook) |
LCC TH9739 .G37 2020 (print) | DDC 621.389/28–dc23
LC record available at https://lccn.loc.gov/2018033599

Printed in China. 1/19

Image Credits

Alamy: David J. Green - electrical, 7 (aluminum tape); Black Rabbit Books:
Grant Gould, 12 (top two); Michael Sellner, 7 (cardboard, battery, buzzer),
8 (buzzers, batteries), 10 (buzzer, cardboard), 11 (buzzers, batteries,
cardboard), 12 (btm), 14 (buzzer, battery, cardboard), 15 (pic),
16 (pic), 17 (pic); Dreamstime: Isaac Marzioli,
Cover (boy), 4 (boy); Shutterstock: Aluna1,
19 (bkgd); Arcady, 7 (sticky note); belka_35,
7 (scissors); durantelallera, Cover ("dring"),
4 ("dring"), 8 ("dring"), 17 shutterstock
("dring"), 23 ("dring"); Galyna G, 14 (bkgd);
Graphic.mooi, Cover (door), 4 (door);
Gurcan Ozkan, 6 (man); Jourdan Laik, 7
(Sharpie); Jumnong, 7 (electrical tape); kaalkop,
21 (camera); mark stay, 18–19 (door);Mega Pixel,
7 (masking tape); Memo Angeles, 2–3 (boy), 17 (girl), 19 (boy); mohinimurti,
Back Cover (bkgd), 4 (bkgd), 16 (bkgd); opicobello, 10 (tear), 14 (tear); Pasko
Maksim, Back Cover (tear), 16 (tear), 23 (top), 24; pitju, 6 (curl), 21 (curl);
Ron Dale, 5 (top), 6 (top), 9, 14 (marker stroke), 16 (marker stroke), 18, 20
(marker stroke); Ron Leishman, Cover (cat), 5 (cat); totallypic, 0 (arrows,
circles), 11 (arrows), 13 (arrow), 16 (arrow); Rasdi Abdul Rahman, 14
(Sharpie); titosart, 20 (btm); Valeriya_Dor, 1; VectorShots, Cover (girl),
4 (girl), 23 (girl)Every effort has been made to contact copyright holders
for material reproduced in this book. Any omissions will be rectified in
subsequent printings if notice is given to the publisher.

Contents

Chapter 1
Get Ready for
Some Fun!

Privacy is important. So is having fun! Making a room alarm is a great way to combine the two. This project comes together in a snap. It uses an electric **circuit**. When an **intruder** enters your room, they'll complete the circuit. Then the alarm will sound. And your stuff will stay safe!

Chapter 2
Let's Build!

Building a room alarm is actually pretty simple. Just gather some supplies, and get started. Don't worry if something doesn't work right away. Experiment until it does. And, most importantly, remember to have fun!

What You'll Need

3-volt battery with wires
(with 1 inch [2.5 centimeters]
of wire **exposed**)

DC3-24V buzzer with
wires (with 1 inch
[2.5 cm] of wire exposed)

electrical
tape

1 5 x 5-inch
(13 x 13-cm) square
of cardboard

1 2 x 2-inch
(5 x 5-cm) square
of aluminum tape

marker

scissors

masking
tape

a **responsible** adult
to help you

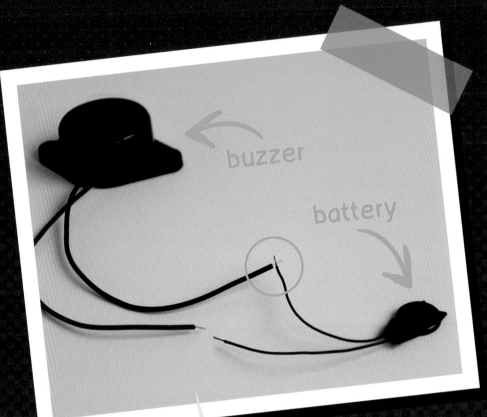

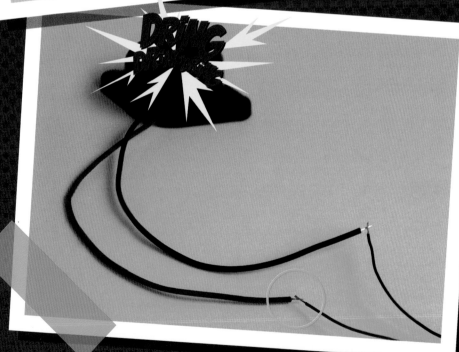

Test the Buzzer and Battery

1 Touch the buzzer's black wire to the battery's black wire.

2 While keeping the black wires together, touch the red wires together. When the wires connect, the buzzer should sound.

3 Once you've tested the buzzer, you can stop holding the wires together.

HINT

An extra set of hands might be helpful. Either grow more hands or have your adult help hold the wires.

Build the Alarm

1 Place the buzzer on the cardboard square near an edge. Center the buzzer. There should be equal amounts of cardboard to the left and right. Its wires should go onto the board.

2 Using masking tape, attach the buzzer to the cardboard.

3 Put the battery on the board directly across from the buzzer. The battery's wires should also extend onto the board.

4 Tape the battery down using masking tape.

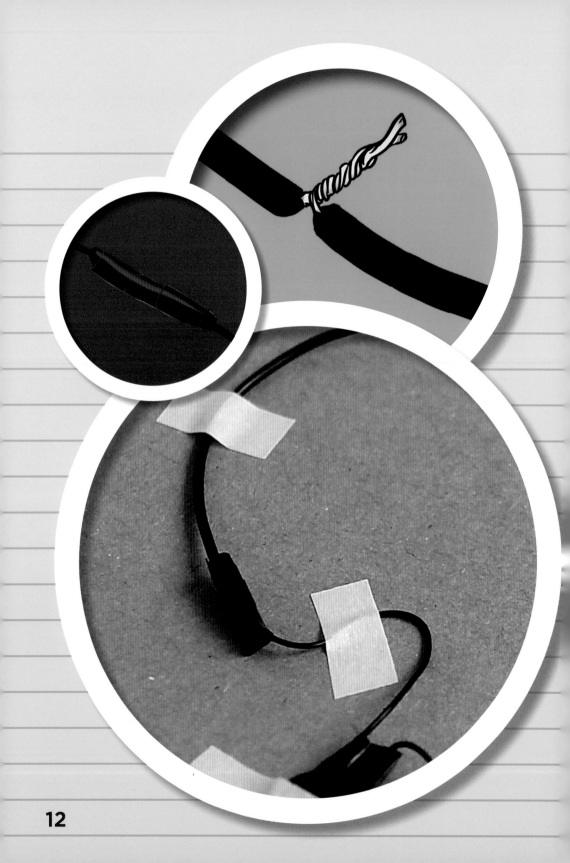

5 Now it's time to work with the buzzer and battery wires. Hold the black wires side by side. Twist the exposed ends together.

6 Bend the twisted wire ends down. Wrap electrical tape around them.

7 Use masking tape to attach the black wires to the cardboard.

8 Straighten out the red wires so they are near each other. Make a mark on the cardboard where each wire ends.

HINT

It's OK if the red wires don't reach each other.

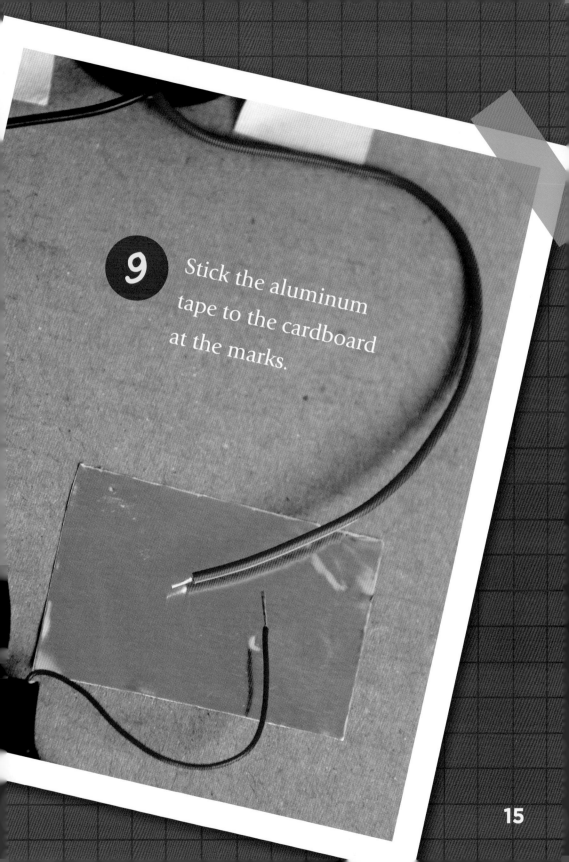

9 Stick the aluminum tape to the cardboard at the marks.

HINT

If the alarm doesn't buzz, double check your circuit. Make sure you're pressing both ends to the tape. If it still doesn't work, check the black wires. Did they come disconnected?

10 Use masking tape to tape down the red wires. Arrange them so their exposed ends hover above the aluminum tape. Do not tape down the exposed ends.

11 Press the two exposed wire ends to the aluminum tape with your finger. The alarm should go off.

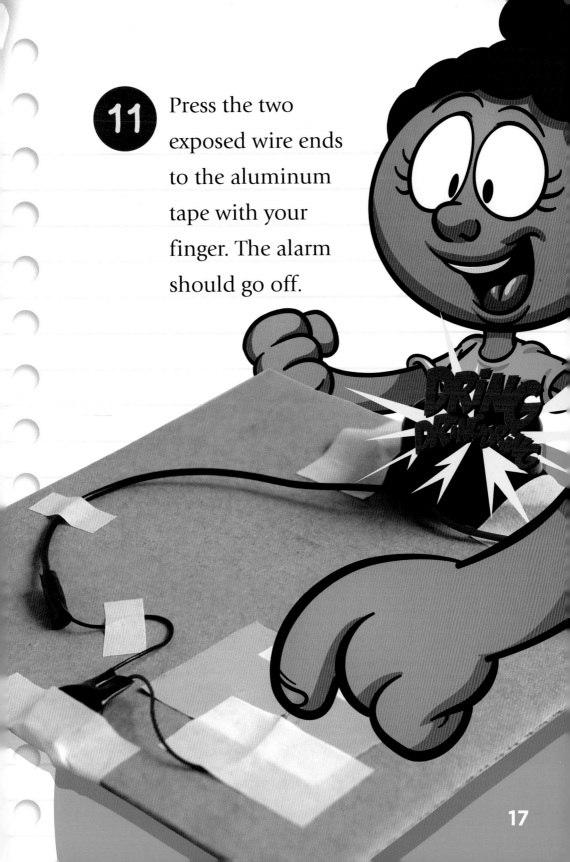

Set the Alarm

Now that your alarm is complete, it's time to set it! Place your alarm under a rug in your room. Now practice walking into your room. Stepping on the alarm should press the wires to the aluminum tape. The buzzer should sound.

HINT Practice walking into your room a few times. These test runs will help you put the alarm in the best place.

Chapter 3
Get in on the
Hi Jinx

You made a simple room alarm using a buzzer and battery. It's just one of many different kinds of alarms. Some alarms are **complex**. They might use motion **sensors**. Others might use video cameras. Maybe you'll make high-tech alarms someday.

Take It One Step More

1. The aluminum tape is a **conductor**. What's its purpose in this alarm?

2. How could you build an alarm for your whole house?

3. How can you increase the chances of someone setting off your alarm?

GLOSSARY

circuit (SUR-kit)—the complete path of an electric current

complex (KOM-pleks)—connected in complicated ways

conductor (kuhn-DUHK-ter)—a material or object that lets electricity or heat move through it

exposed (ek-SPOZD)—not covered

intruder (in-TROOD-uhr)—someone or something that comes or goes into a place where they are not wanted or welcome

privacy (PRAHY-vuh-see)—the state of being away or private from others

responsible (ri-SPON-suh-buhl)— able to be trusted to do what is right or to do things that are expected or required

sensor (SEN-sor)—a device that finds heat, light, sound, motion, or other things

LEARN MORE

BOOKS

Glendening, Mary, and Isaac Glendening. *Makerspace Sound and Music Projects for All Ages.* New York: McGraw-Hill Education, 2017.

Holzweiss, Kristina A. *Amazing Makerspace DIY with Electricity.* A True Book. New York: Children's Press, an imprint of Scholastic Inc., 2018.

Staley, Erin. *10 Great Makerspace Projects Using Science.* Using Makerspaces for School Projects. New York: Rosen Publishing, 2018.

WEBSITES

Designing Electric Circuits: Door Alarm
www.pbslearningmedia.org/ resource/phy03.sci.phys.mfw. zalarm/designing-electric- circuits-door-alarm/

Electrical Circuits for Kids
www.dkfindout.com/us/ science/electricity/circuits/

Room Alarm
www.instructables.com/id/ Room-Alarm/

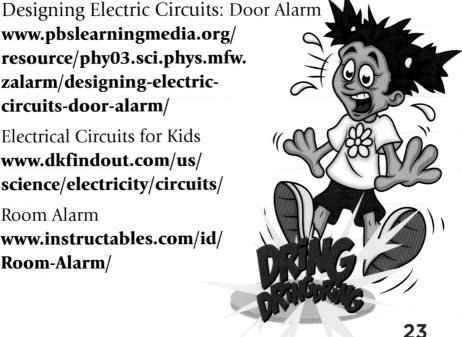

Don't be afraid to ask your adult for help. Some steps can be tricky.

It's OK if your wires' ends aren't exposed. Use a wire stripper to take off as much casing as needed. (Have your adult help with this process.)

If you don't have a rug, try using a piece of clothing.

Planting more alarms will increase the chances of someone setting one off. Make some more alarms for maximum security!